CAREERS IN THE
BUILDING TRADES

A GROWING DEMAND

Carpenter

Careers in the Building Trades

A Growing Demand

 Apprenticeships

 Carpenter

 Construction & Building Inspector

 Electrician

 Flooring Installer

 Heating and Cooling Technician

 Masonry Worker

 Plumber

 Roofer

Working in Green Construction

CAREERS IN THE
BUILDING TRADES

A GROWING DEMAND

Carpenter

Andrew Morkes

MASON CREST

Mason Crest
450 Parkway Drive, Suite D
Broomall, Pennsylvania 19008
(866) MCP-BOOK (toll-free)
www.masoncrest.com

First printing

9 8 7 6 5 4 3 2 1
ISBN (hardback) 978-1-4222-4112-7

ISBN (series) 978-1-4222-4110-3

ISBN (ebook) 978-1-4222-7682-2

Cataloging-in-Publication Data on file with the Library of Congress

Developed and Produced by National Highlights Inc.
Proofreader: Mika Jin
Interior and cover design: Yolanda Van Cooten
Production: Michelle Luke

QR CODES AND LINKS TO THIRD-PARTY CONTENT
You may gain access to certain third-party content ("Third-Party Sites") by scanning and using the QR Codes that appear in this publication (the "QR Codes"). We do not operate or control in any respect any information, products, or services on such Third-Party Sites linked to by us via the QR Codes included in this publication, and we assume no responsibility for any materials you may access using the QR Codes. Your use of the QR Codes may be subject to terms, limitations, or restrictions set forth in the applicable terms of use or otherwise established by the owners of the Third-Party Sites. Our linking to such Third-Party Sites via the QR Codes does not imply an endorsement or sponsorship of such Third-Party Sites or the information, products, or services offered on or through the Third-Party Sites, nor does it imply an endorsement or sponsorship of this publication by the owners of such Third-Party Sites.

CONTENTS

KEY ICONS TO LOOK FOR:

Words to understand: These words with their easy-to-understand definitions will increase the reader's understanding of the text while building vocabulary skills.

Sidebars: This boxed material within the main text allows readers to build knowledge, gain insights, explore possibilities, and broaden their perspectives by weaving together additional information to provide realistic and holistic perspectives.

Educational Videos: Readers can view videos by scanning our QR codes, providing them with additional educational content to supplement the text. Examples include news coverage, moments in history, speeches, iconic sports moments and much more!

Text-dependent questions: These questions send the reader back to the text for more careful attention to the evidence presented there.

Research projects: Readers are pointed toward areas of further inquiry connected to each chapter. Suggestions are provided for projects that encourage deeper research and analysis.

Series glossary of key terms: This back-of-the-book glossary contains terminology used throughout this series. Words found here increase the reader's ability to read and comprehend higher-level books and articles in this field.

INTRODUCTION

The Trades: Great Careers, Good Money, and Other Rewards

Trades workers play a major role in the success of economies throughout the world. They build structures ranging from houses to skyscrapers, keep the power on, and install and repair pipes that carry water, fuel, and other liquids to, from, and within businesses, factories, and homes, among many other job duties. Yet despite their pivotal role in our society, only 6 percent of students consider a career in the trades, according to ExploretheTrades.org. Why? Because many young people have misconceptions about the trades. They have been told that the trades are low-paying, lack job security, and other untruths. In fact, working in the trades is one of the best career choices you can make. The following paragraphs provide more information on why a career in the trades is a good idea.

Good pay. Contrary to public perception, skilled trades workers earn salaries that place them firmly in the middle class. For example, median annual salaries for carpenters in the United States are $44,689, according to PayScale.com. This salary is roughly equal to or higher than the median earnings for some careers that require a bachelor's or graduate degree—including event planners ($44,921), social workers ($44,577), mental health counselors ($40,244), and recreational therapists ($38,958). Trades workers who become managers or who launch their own businesses can have earnings that range from $90,000 to $200,000.

Strong employment prospects. There are shortages of trades workers throughout the world, according to the human resource consulting firm ManpowerGroup. In fact,

trades workers are the most in-demand occupational field in the Americas, Europe, the Middle East, and Africa. They ranked fourth in the Asia-Pacific region.

Provides a comfortable life without a bachelor's or graduate degree. For decades in the United States and other countries, there has been an emphasis on earning a college degree as the key to life success. But studies show that only 35 percent of future jobs in the U.S. will require a four-year degree or higher. With college tuition continuing to increase and the chances of landing a good job out of college decreasing, a growing number of people are entering apprenticeship programs to prepare for careers in the trades. And unlike college students, apprentices receive a salary while learning and they don't have to pay off loans after they complete their education. It's a good feeling to start your career without $50,000 to $200,000 in college loans.

Rewarding work environment and many career options. A career in the trades is fulfilling because you get to use both your hands and your head to solve problems and make the world a better place. You can work at a construction site, at a manufacturing plant, at a business, and in other settings. Many trades workers launch their own businesses.

Jobs can't be offshored. Trades careers involve hands-on work that requires the worker to be on-site to do his or her job. As a result, there is no chance that your position will be offshored to a foreign country. In an uncertain employment atmosphere, that's encouraging news.

Job opportunities are available throughout the United States and the world. There is a need for trades workers in small towns and big cities. If demand for their skills is not strong in their geographic area, they can move to other cities, states, or countries where demand is higher.

Are the Trades Right for Me?

Test your interest in the trades. How many of these statements do you agree with?

- ☐ **My favorite class in school is shop.**

- ☐ **I enjoy woodworking.**

- ☐ **I like doing household repairs.**

- ☐ **I like to use power and hand tools.**

- ☐ **I like projects that allow me to work with my hands.**

- ☐ **I enjoy observing work at construction sites.**

- ☐ **I like to build and fix things.**

- ☐ **I like to watch home-repair shows on TV and the internet.**

- ☐ **I don't mind getting my hands dirty.**

- ☐ **I like solving problems.**

- ☐ **I am good at math.**

- ☐ **I like to figure out how things work.**

If many of the statements above describe you, then you should consider a career in the trades. But you don't need to select a career right now. Check out this book on a career as a carpenter and other books in the series to learn more about occupational paths in the trades. Good luck with your career exploration!

■ *About 55 percent of carpenters in the United States work in the construction industry.*

Words to Understand

civil engineering: An engineering specialty that focuses on the design, construction, and maintenance of roads, buildings, dams, bridges, airports, tunnels, and water and sewage treatment systems.

computer-aided design software: Software that allows users to draw artwork or blueprints on a computer.

condominium: A building with residential or business units that are individually owned, but which also features common areas (laundry, swimming pool, fitness room, etc.) that are owned by all unit owners.

self-employed: Working for oneself as a small business owner, rather than for a corporation or other employer. Self-employed people must generate their own income and provide their own fringe benefits (such as health insurance).

CHAPTER 1

What Do Carpenters Do?

Some people take carpenters for granted, but without them, we would not have nice homes, superhighways, and stunning skyscrapers. And let's not forget the well-crafted cabinets, tables, and other furniture that add beauty to our homes and offices. Carpenters are jacks-of-all-trades who not only work with wood, but also with plastic, metal, fiberglass, drywall, and other building materials. They do everything from erecting scaffolding and building concrete forms, to assembling walls and building stairs, to installing cabinets and countertops and crafting high-quality furniture. They work in residential settings, at construction sites, and on big infrastructure projects such as highways and bridges. Carpenters are in the middle of the action wherever something is being built.

Carpenters work for construction companies and contractors. Others operate their own businesses. To hone their skills and experience, aspiring carpenters complete apprenticeships or training programs at technical schools. Others receive informal training from experienced carpenters, or through contractor schools or the military.

■ *A team of rough carpenters raise an interior wall at a construction site.*

The job of carpenter often ranks high on "best construction occupation" lists. Carpenters agree that this is the perfect career for those who like to build things, who

Hardwood or Softwood?

Do you know that the terms *softwood* and *hardwood* don't pertain to the softness or hardness of the wood on a tree? They actually refer to the leaves, seeds, and structure of the tree. Here's a closer look at hardwood and softwood, and how to tell the difference.

Hardwood is wood that comes from trees (known as deciduous trees) that typically lose their broad leaves in the fall. Examples include oak, birch, mahogany, teak, walnut, maple, and hickory. Because hardwood lasts longer and is more difficult to work with, it is more expensive.

Softwood is wood that comes from trees (known as coniferous trees) that have triangular shapes and needle-like leaves that are either long and pointed or long and flat-scaled. They do not lose their needles in the fall, but will shed a few when new needles are ready. Examples include pine, cedars, firs, cypress, juniper, spruce, and redwoods. Softwood is easier to work with and less expensive, and is often used for doors and flooring in homes.

enjoy a constantly-changing and rewarding work environment, and the opportunity to make a good living without earning a four-year degree.

■ *A carpenter discusses his job duties, necessary skills, and work environment.*

Types of Carpenters

There are two basic types of carpenters: *rough carpenters* and *finish carpenters.* Rough carpenters, who are also known as *structural carpenters,* construct the inner frameworks of building and temporary structures (scaffolds, forms in which concrete is poured into, bridge or sewer supports, etc.) by following blueprints or oral instructions from foremen and construction superintendents. They help build or repair homes, apartment buildings, factories, bridges, roads, railroads, airports, or any other type of structure imaginable. It is extremely important that their work is of the utmost quality. Otherwise, buildings under construction may collapse or may not be built up to code. Typical duties of rough carpenters include:

- Studying blueprints, sketches, or building plans, or following supervisor instructions, to prepare the project layout and determine dimensions and the types of lumber, materials, supplies, and tools that are required

- Using hand tools, power tools, and machines to shape or cut wood, plastic, and other materials

- Constructing forms or chutes for pouring concrete

- Erecting scaffolding or ladders for assembling structures

- Constructing and erecting building frameworks, including floors, walls, and doorframes

- Installing components and fixtures such as windows, doors, and molding

- Installing insulation or drywall

- Installing roof joists, trusses, and rafters

- Laying roofs with shingles and plywood

- Laying wood floors and stairs

- Installing weather-stripping, insulation, and caulking

- Installing drywall

- Removing damaged or defective components or sections of structures and repairing or replacing them

- Checking completed work with squares or levels

- Performing minor welding, plumbing, electrical, or concrete mixing work.

■ *A finish carpentry apprentice completes work on a dresser.*

A career as a rough carpenter is a good fit if you like working as a member of a team, enjoy having a wide range of job duties, don't mind working outdoors in all types of weather, and are willing to work at night and on weekends to keep projects on schedule. This career involves travel to job sites, so you'll need a driver's license and a trustworthy vehicle.

Rough carpenters may further specialize. *Residential carpenters* focus on building and remodeling single-family homes, townhomes, and **condominiums**. Commercial carpenters build and remodel office buildings, schools, shopping malls, casinos, hospitals, and hotels. *Industrial carpenters* typically work on **civil engineering** projects (such as roads, bridges, marinas, etc.) and in industrial settings (manufacturing plants, etc.).

Finish carpenters, who are also known as *detail carpenters,* build and install cabinets, shelves, stairs, and floors that are made of wood, wood substitutes, and other materials. They are highly skilled crafts workers who primarily work indoors in workshops or in the homes or offices of customers. Unlike rough carpenters—who often work at night and on weekends—finish carpenters enjoy a standard nine-to-five, Monday through Friday schedule, unless they choose to work extra hours to earn more money or build their client base. Major duties of finish carpenters include:

- Meeting with customers or construction foremen or superintendents to discuss the work in question and develop a plan of action
- Repairing or altering cabinetry, wooden furniture, fixtures, paneling, or other wood components per project specifications
- Using **computer-aided design software** or hand-drawn diagrams to create blueprints for new furniture or other components
- Using paint, lacquers, or specially-created trim to finish the surfaces of woodwork or wallboard in houses or other buildings
- Applying sound-deadening or decorative paneling to walls or ceilings
- Using hand tools, power tools, and machines to cut, mold, or shape wood or wood substitutes
- Using glue, nails, screws, dowels, or clamps to attach parts, components, or subassemblies
- Installing hardware such as handles, hinges, catches, or drawer pulls
- Trimming, sanding, scraping or otherwise preparing parts or components for finishing
- Applying stain, paint, varnish, or lacquer to complete products.

If you have artistic ability, are attentive to detail, have a patient personality, and desire a standard nine-to-five work schedule, a career as a finish carpenter will be a good fit.

Carpenters are multiskilled professionals. It is not uncommon for rough carpenters to obtain additional training and skills to also be qualified to perform finish carpentry. And finish carpenters may also do rough carpentry if business is slow.

■ *Check out carpenters working in a variety of jobs.*

Becoming a Boss

After a few years on the job, skilled carpenters with leadership potential can be promoted to the position of *foreman*. These mid-level managers supervise a team of carpenters and apprentices as they build homes, highways, bridges, and other structures. Major job responsibilities for foremen include:

- Ensuring that crews meet project deadlines

- Occasionally helping carpenters and apprentices to complete tasks that range from building forms for concrete, to installing doors and windows, to cutting and shaping timbers for floorboards

- Checking finished work to make sure that it meets applicable building codes and project specifications

- Meeting with project superintendents throughout the project to ensure that the work is being completed on-budget, on-time, and meeting other project guidelines

- Assessing the work of apprentices as they do their jobs to ensure that their skills and construction knowledge are improving.

The career of foreman is a good fit for those who enjoy managing others, travelling to multiple construction sites to supervise work teams, and occasionally working at night and on weekends to meet project deadlines. The job can be stressful if you

They Were Carpenters!?

Did you know that Harrison Ford worked as a carpenter before achieving fame as Han Solo in *Star Wars*? In 1970, he was hired to build a music studio for Brazilian jazz star Sérgio Mendes—who did not know it was Ford's first time working as a carpenter. Ford recalls that he learned carpentry by checking out books from the local public library. In his roughly eight years as a carpenter, Ford also did

■ *The well-known actor Mark Harmon once worked as a carpenter.*

carpentry work for the actresses Valerie Harper and Sally Kellerman and became known as the "carpenter to the stars." Here are a few other well-known people who worked as carpenters before becoming successful in another field:

- **Bernie Sanders** briefly worked as a carpenter before becoming the mayor of Burlington, Vermont, a senator from Vermont, and a presidential candidate.

- College football star and award-winning actor **Mark Harmon** says that if he wasn't an actor, he would be a carpenter. Harmon worked briefly as a carpenter before he became famous, but found it hard to get steady work.

- **Nick Offerman,** one of the stars of *Parks and Recreation,* loves woodworking and carpentry. In addition to acting, he owns a woodworking shop that creates and sells everything from tables and benches, to canoes and lamps.

Sources: Entertainment Tonight, Men's Health, Vanity Fair

■ *A foreman (left) reviews measurements with an apprentice.*

don't like constant travel and the pressure of managing workers and producing results for your bosses.

Starting Your Own Contracting Business

Nearly 34 percent of carpenters in the United States are **self-employed**, according to the U.S. Department of Labor. That's much higher than the average (10.1 percent) for people in all careers. Self-employed workers, known as contractors, oversee businesses that range in size from one person to a team of carpenters and office staff. Carpentry contractors provide services to homeowners, businesses, nonprofit organizations, and government agencies. Most contractors work for residential customers. Contractors help new homeowners remodel kitchens or bathrooms—or entire homes. They build decks, garages, and sheds, as well as ramps to help those with disabilities more easily access buildings. They replace or repair cabinets, floors, windows, doors, stairs, trim, and moldings. In short, they repair or build anything that is structural in nature. Most carpenters leave the plumbing, heating and cooling, and electrical work

■ *A contractor (left) and one of his employees work on a door in a customer's home.*

to those who are skilled in these areas. But some carpenters also have expertise in these specialties. These talents allow them to attract even more customers.

There are many reasons why it's rewarding to be a carpentry contractor. For one, you get to be your own boss—deciding what type of customers you'll cater to, what rates you'll charge, when you'll work, and much more. If your business is successful, you'll make a lot more money than the average carpenter.

On the other hand, it's challenging to be a business owner. One carpenter describes his business in the following way: "I'm the captain of my ship, but I also have to be the wind and the sail." This means that you not only have to do the actual carpentry work, but you need to run your business and always be looking for new customers. You'll spend hours each week managing office staff, billing customers and tracking down those who don't pay their bills, promoting your business through word-of-mouth, newspaper ads, and even social media, and performing many other tasks. Working as a contractor is not easy, but it can be both personally and financially rewarding.

■ *Learn more about the variety of job duties for carpenters, required skills, salaries, and training.*

Staying Safe on the Job

Carpenters have one of the highest rates of injuries and illnesses of all careers, according to the U.S. Department of Labor. Some accidents are even fatal, but that number is small given the large number of carpenters who are employed in the construction and home remodeling industries. The most common injuries to carpenters include:

■ *Carpenters wear safety harnesses and other protective gear when working at great heights.*

- Wounds, lacerations, and amputations to fingers and hands from protruding nails and other sharp objects, nail guns, and injuries incurred while sawing/cutting
- Falls from ladders
- Back injury and muscle stress/strain
- Knee/leg injuries caused by kneeling for long periods or slipping on wet or icy surfaces.

Other injuries, fatalities, and health conditions are caused by flying objects; exposure to dust, chemicals, and hazardous fumes; fires and explosions; extremely hot or cold weather; repetitive movements; molds and fungi; loud noises from machinery and tools; and electrocution.

Carpenters follow many safety practices to avoid injuries, and even death. They wear heavy gloves, steel-toed work shoes, and other protective clothing. They also use safety equipment such as hardhats, hearing protection, face shields, respirators, and body harnesses. Here are a few safety measures to follow if you work as a carpenter:

- Be sure the power is turned off when working near electrical outlets or other electrical components.
- Be extremely careful on ladders or when working at heights. Many carpenters wear safety harnesses and other protective gear in these situations.
- Never operate machinery without safety guards in place.
- Be sure that your own equipment works properly. Check for frayed electrical cords, damaged power tools, and other issues that might put you in danger on the job.
- Always ventilate rooms when working with paints, lacquers, or finishes with hazardous solvents. Use fans to circulate the air, and, ideally, wear a respirator.
- Be careful when lifting heavy materials or tools. Ask another carpenter to assist you if building materials are too heavy.
- Address your concerns about project safety with your foreman or the job superintendent.

Text-Dependent Questions

1. What type of carpenters build furniture?

2. What are some of the best aspects of a career as a carpentry contractor?

3. What kinds of safety gear do carpenters use to protect themselves?

Research Project

Visit https://www.youtube.com/watch?v=PRwi9lzqzMU to learn how to build your own birdhouse. Once you complete your first birdhouse, teach friends and family how to do so, too.

CHAPTER 2

Tools of the Trade

Cutting, Bending, Extracting, Smoothing, & Shaping Tools

awl: A sharp hand tool that is used to make holes in wood and soft materials such as leather.

chisel: A hand tool with a shaped, sharp cutting edge that is used to cut, chip, or carve wood, metal, or stone.

circular saw: A power saw with a round flat blade that is used to cut wood, plastic, metal, or other building materials.

drill: A hand or power tool that is fitted with a cutting tool attachment or driving tool attachment; it is used to cut into material ranging from wood and stone, to metal and plastic.

hand saw: A cutting tool with a long, thin serrated steel blade; it is operated using a backward and forward movement.

plane: A hand tool that is used to smooth and reduce the thickness of wood surfaces.

pliers: A hand tool that is used to hold objects firmly, as well as bend and compress a variety of materials.

power saw: A cutting device that is battery- or electric-powered.

router: A power tool that is used to cut cabinet joints, shape decorative edges, trim laminate, and perform other steps in the construction process.

sander: A power tool that uses sandpaper or other abrasive material to smooth a surface.

Joining Tools

hammer: A hand tool with a metal or wooden head that is mounted to the handle at right angles; it is used to drive or remove nails or break-up old construction materials.

nail gun: A power tool that is used to quickly drive nails into wood or other construction materials.

screwdriver: A manual or powered device that turns screws; available with a flattened, cross-shaped style (known as a flathead screwdriver), or with a star-shaped tip that fits into the head of a screw to turn it (often referred to as a Phillips® screwdriver).

Measuring Tools

framing square: A measuring device that has a long arm and a shorter arm, which intersect at a right angle (90 degrees); it is used as a guide when carpenters draw lines on materials before cutting, or for locating holes. Also known as a **carpenter's square**.

laser measure: A device that allows users to take distance measurements instantly.

level: A device that is used to establish a horizontal plane. It is comprised of a small glass tube that contains alcohol or a similar liquid and an air bubble.

tape measure: A flexible ruler made up of fiber glass, a metal strip, cloth, or plastic.

Computer Technology

building information modeling software: A computer application that uses a 3D model-based process that helps construction, architecture, and engineering professionals to more efficiently plan, design, build, and manage buildings and infrastructure.

office management software: A computer application that helps users track finances and manage billing, draft correspondence, and perform other tasks.

CHAPTER 3

Terms of the Trade

adhesive: A substance such as glue or contact cement that can be used to bond material together by surface attachment.

beam: A structural element made of wood, stone, metal, or a combination of wood and metal that supports one or more joists.

blueprints: A reproduction of a technical plan for the construction of a home or other structure. Blueprints are created by licensed architects.

building codes: A series of rules established by local, state, regional, and national governments that ensure safe construction. The National Electrical Code, which was developed by the National Fire Protection Association, is an example of a building code in the United States.

ceiling joist: A construction component that connects the outside walls, supports the ceiling for the room below, and secures the bottom ends of the rafters. If one views the roof structure as an equilateral triangle, the rafters would make up the top left and right segments of the triangle, and the ceiling joist the bottom segment.

finish carpentry: Carpentry work that is completed after the structural carpentry work is finished; this type of carpentry involves woodwork—such as cabinetry, fine woodworking, joinery, and parquetry—that can be seen by the homeowner or other customer. Also known as trim carpentry.

foundation: In a construction project, the part of the structure that connects it to the ground and evenly distributes the weight of the structure.

framing carpentry: Measuring, cutting, and assembling wood and other materials to create the basic framework for floor, wall, and roof framing, window installation, and exterior door installation. Also known as rough carpentry.

green construction: The planning, design, construction, and operation of structures in an environmentally responsible manner. Green construction stresses energy and water efficiency, the use of eco-friendly construction materials (when possible), indoor environmental quality, and the structure's overall effects on its site or the larger community. Also known as green building.

joists: A series of parallel, horizontal components of wood, engineered wood, or steel that support a ceiling or floor. Joists are supported by beams, wall framing, and foundations.

layout: A step during the early phases of a construction project in which a carpenter uses blueprints and instructions from the construction manager to measure and mark (using a chalk line or other marking device) work that he or she will do during the project.

load-bearing wall: A wall that is typically constructed of sturdy materials (such as brick, concrete, or block) that serves as a support for other components of the structure. Also called a bearing wall.

non-load-bearing wall: A wall that does not provide significant support for any components above it. Also called a curtain wall.

pitch: In construction, the angle of rise in degrees from a horizontal starting point. The degree of pitch is an important consideration in staircase and roof construction because it affects the type of construction materials that are used, water drainage considerations, and the amount of room in the upper story or attic of a building.

plumb: Slang for a wall, post, beam, or other structure that is perfectly vertical.

primary wood: Visually-appealing wood (such as oak and mahogany) that is used in areas of construction or in the exterior of furniture that will be seen by the end-user.

proud: Slang for when one building component protrudes above another.

punch list: A list that details what needs to be done during a construction project. Also known as a snag list.

rafter: A sloping framing component that runs downward from the peak of the roof to the ceiling joist. If one views the roof structure as an equilateral triangle, the rafters would make up the top left and right segments of the triangle, and the ceiling joist the bottom segment.

sawhorse: A wood or metal beam with four legs. Two or more sawhorses are used in tandem to support a board or plank to make it easier to saw or perform other construction tasks.

schematic diagram: An illustration of the components of a system that uses abstract, graphic symbols instead of realistic pictures or illustrations.

secondary wood: Less-expensive and less-attractive wood (such as poplar, soft maple, pine, and plywood) that is used to complete areas that are not seen after the project is completed. Examples include the dust dividers, bracing, nailing cleats, and drawer sides in furniture.

truss: A structural framework of wood that serves to bridge the space above a room and support the roof.

wall framing: Fitting together pieces of wood and other building materials to construct a wall.

wall stud: Vertical wood or metal beams that support the actual wall in a structure. They are spaced either 16 or 24 inches (406.4000 millimeters or 609.6000 millimeters) on-center along the wall and span from the floor to ceiling. Heavy objects such as large pictures and shelves should be anchored in studs because the regular wall is not strong enough to support their weight.

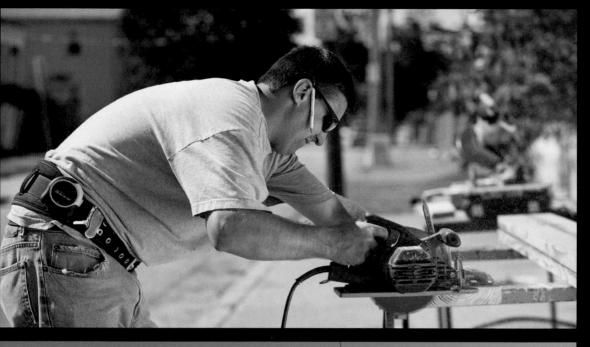

■ *Participating in an apprenticeship is the most-common educational path for carpenters.*

Words to Understand

apprenticeship: A formal training program that combines classroom instruction and supervised practical experience. Apprentices are paid a salary that increases as they obtain experience.

community college: A private or public two-year college that awards certificates and associate degrees.

technical college: A public or private college that offers two- or four-year programs in practical subjects, such as the trades, information technology, applied sciences, agriculture, and engineering.

union: An organization that seeks to gain better wages, benefits, and working conditions for its members. Also called a **labor union** or **trade union**.

CHAPTER 4

Preparing for the Field and Making a Living

Educational Paths

There are several ways to learn how to become a carpenter. You can participate in an apprenticeship (the most popular entry method), attend college, learn through informal methods such as working as a helper to an experienced carpenter, or receive training in the military. Regardless of your educational path, you'll need to be dedicated and work hard to achieve your goals. Many people want to become carpenters.

High School Classes

Several high school classes will help you to prepare for a career as a carpenter. Shop and woodworking classes are the most important because they will help you to get hands-on experience with tools and machinery and building projects. Woodworking classes are offered as part of shop curriculum, or as separate classes. In a woodworking class, you'll learn:

■ *Take as many mathematics classes as possible in high school because carpenters use their math skills every day.*

- The types of wood and their characteristics and properties
- How to use hand and power tools, and their various applications
- How to use woodworking stationary machines such as miter saws, drill presses, band saws, dovetail machines, lathes, and power sanders
- How to use safety gear
- How to draw up building plans and estimate project costs
- Woodworking and cabinetmaking styles and techniques
- Finishing processes and techniques.

Some schools offer specialized curricula in carpentry. These programs will expand on what you learned in shop or woodworking classes. You'll also learn about rough framing and the building permitting and inspection process, and how to use ladders

■ *An instructor teaches an apprentice how to use a saw.*

and scaffolding, among other topics. In some programs, you might even get the opportunity to leave the school campus to work on construction projects such as decks, garages, home additions, and new homes.

Take mathematics classes because carpenters use basic math to calculate wall heights, floor space, the length of rafters, and spindle spacings, as well as trigonometry to make right angle cuts. If you own your own business, you'll use math to calculate estimates, manage payroll, and for other business-related tasks.

If you plan to become a business owner, be sure to take business, accounting, marketing, and English/writing classes. A foreign language such as Spanish will come in handy if you work with or for people who do not speak English as a first language. Don't forget computer science classes or any courses that introduce you to technology. Carpenters use digital devices for measuring, tablet computers to review blueprints, and computers, apps, and other technology to track customer appointments, keep records, perform basic accounting, and write and post advertisements about their businesses on the internet and social media.

■ *Learn about the benefits of training via an apprenticeship program.*

Pre-Apprenticeships

Some people participate in pre-apprenticeship programs before entering an apprenticeship program. For example, the Carpenters Training Committee for Northern California in the United States offers a six-week program that combines both classroom and shop training. Participants learn construction math and spend a lot of time in the shop building projects. Completion of the pre-apprenticeship program is required to enter the committee's apprenticeship program.

The National Association of Home Builders offers pre-apprenticeship certificate training through the Home Builders Institute. The program is geared toward high school and college students, transitioning military members, veterans, justice-involved youth and adults, and unemployed and displaced workers. Programs are available in carpentry, building construction technology, weatherization, electrical, plumbing, landscaping, masonry, and painting. In the Carpentry Program, students learn how to build forms for concrete; build walls; install doors, windows, and siding; lay wood floors and stairs; install cabinets and countertops; install interior finish and trim; use green building techniques to conserve energy and increase durability of structures; and much more.

■ *Learn more about the ins and outs of participating in an apprenticeship.*

Apprenticeships

Most people prepare to become carpenters by completing an apprenticeship program, which typically lasts three to four years. In the United States, trainees complete 2,000 hours of on-the-job training and 144 hours of related classroom instruction during each year in the program.

Apprenticeship programs are offered by regional and district councils (in the U.S. and Canada) of the United Brotherhood of Carpenters and Joiners of America; Associated Builders and Contractors; Timber Framers Guild; and other organizations. Entry requirements vary by program, but typical requirements include:

Carpenter Career Path

Hard work and talent is rewarded in the trades. With a few years of hard work, you can advance to managerial positions or even start your own contracting business. Here is a typical career ladder for carpenters.

Business Owner: Operates a contracting firm that provides carpentry services to homeowners and businesses.

Project Superintendent: Oversees work for entire projects; is responsible for staffing, ordering supplies and equipment, quality control, and other tasks.

Foreman: A journeyman carpenter who manages a group of other journeymen and apprentices on a project.

Journeyman Carpenter: Has completed apprenticeship training. If licensed, can work by him- or herself without direct supervision, but, for large projects, must work under permits issued to a contracting firm owner.

Apprentice Carpenter: Apprentice carpenters in the United States complete 2,000 hours of on-the-job training and 144 hours of related classroom instruction during a three- or four-year course of study. Program lengths and requirements vary by country.

■ *A superintendent discusses a project with one of his workers.*

- Minimum age of eighteen
- High school education
- One year of high school algebra
- Qualifying score on an aptitude test
- Drug free

The United Brotherhood of Carpenters and Joiners of America (which is known as the UBC) offers continuing education classes and programs, superintendent training opportunities, and experiential/training programs for third-year apprentices at its International Training Center.

Visit http://www.doleta.gov/OA/sainformation.cfm for information on apprenticeship training programs in the United States. If you live in another country, contact your nation's department of labor to learn more about training programs.

As you move through the apprentice program, you'll expand your skills, gain valuable hands-on experience, and receive higher wages. Those who complete a carpentry apprenticeship training program are known as *journeymen carpenters*. Carpenters who work as contractors must be licensed in most U.S. states. The requirements vary by state. Licensing requirements vary in other countries; departments of labor or licensing can provide more information.

Technical and Community College

Some aspiring carpenters choose to prepare for the field by earning a certificate and/or an associate degree in carpentry, woodworking, or general construction from a **technical college** or **community college**. Many of these degree programs are affiliated with **unions** or contractor organizations. These programs feature a combination of classwork, shop work, and hands-on experience via an internship or informal apprenticeship with a construction firm. Typical classes in a carpentry associate degree program include:

- Elements of Construction
- Foundations and Forms Construction
- Rough Framing
- Stair Building and Framing

- Roof Framing
- Residential Plumbing for Carpenters
- Residential Electrical for Carpenters
- Construction Rehabilitation: Kitchens and Baths
- Construction Estimating
- Residential Projects

■ *A student uses a circular saw in a community college carpentry class.*

Which Educational Path Is Best for Me?

We've discussed the variety of ways to become a carpenter. But which is best? The answer is that no path is more right than another. Each has its pros and cons, and you need to select the strategy that works best for your learning style, personality, and employment goals. Here's a breakdown of your options and the pros and cons:

Apprenticeship

Pros: The most popular preparation method because it provides a clear path to employment. Completion of an apprenticeship looks great on a resume. You receive a salary that increases as you gain experience.

Con: Programs last three to four years.

A Good Fit: For those who like a structured environment that combines both classroom and hands-on training.

Technical School/Community College

Pros: Programs are shorter than apprenticeships—typically one to two years.

Cons: You must pay tuition and you do not receive pay like apprentices do.

A Good Fit: For those who want to enter the workforce more quickly.

Informal Training

Pros: Allows you to get to work right away and receive a salary.

Cons: Training might not be as detailed as an apprenticeship or degree program.

A Good Fit: For those who do not need a structured educational setting to learn and who are able to pick up their skills and knowledge on the job.

Military Training

Pros: You receive quality training and a salary.

Cons: You will be required to serve your country for two or more years anyplace in the world, including in a war zone.

A Good Fit: For those who respect authority, can follow instructions, and have a disciplined personality.

- Residential Building Codes for Carpenters
- Technical Mathematics with Algebra
- Technical Mathematics with Geometry
- Introduction to the Skilled Trades.

Informal Training Opportunities

Some carpenters learn their skills by working for three to five years as carpenter helpers at a construction site or for a self-employed carpenter. In the beginning, you'll probably just carry tools and building materials back and forth, erect scaffolding. and clean work areas. As you gain experience (and some formal training at a technical school), your duties will expand and you'll be asked to cut timbers, lumber, or paneling; measure and cut wooden and metal studs; construct forms; and perform finishing work.

Military

The career of carpenter is probably not the first occupation that comes to mind when you think of jobs in the military. But militaries around the world need carpenters to help build temporary and permanent structures, and repair bridges, foundations,

■ *An Army carpenter cuts a 2x12 board for a wooden hut at a training area.*

buildings, dams, and bunkers. All five U.S. military branches (Air Force, Army, Coast Guard, Marines, Navy), as well as many militaries in other countries, provide training for carpenters. According to TodaysMilitary.com, job training in the U.S. military branches "consists of instruction, including practice with carpentry and masonry tools. Further training occurs on the job and through advanced courses." In the military, you'll learn building construction techniques, masonry construction methods, types and uses of construction joints and braces, cabinetmaking, and how to mix and set concrete, mortar, and plaster.

While you train, you'll receive a salary and will not have to pay any tuition, but you will have to make a service commitment of two to four years. Ask your recruiter for more information.

One caveat: the military will not promise you a job as a carpenter when you enlist. It assigns you where it needs you—whether that's on the front lines of a war, driving a truck, or working in an office.

Other Training Opportunities

Some large contractors operate their own training programs. While they are not recognized apprenticeship programs, they provide similar classroom and on-the-job instruction. Contact contractors in your area regarding potential training opportunities.

■ *A female apprentice talks about the rewards and challenges of participating in an apprenticeship.*

Getting a Job

You've completed your training. Now you're a journeyman carpenter. But how do you get a job? You might already have a job lined up through your apprenticeship program or your college's career services office, but, if not, you'll have to look for a job. Here are some popular job-search strategies:

Use Your Network. Have you heard of networking? If not, it's just a way to trade information with others who are seeking a job. Your professional network consists of fellow apprentices and classmates, job superintendents, instructors, and even your family or friends who know people in the construction industry. You can network at industry events (such as job fairs), in casual settings such as after-work get-togethers with friends and co-workers or family barbeques, on the telephone, via email, or on social networking sites such as LinkedIn. The goal of networking is to learn about potential employers and job opportunities and tell as many people as possible that you're looking for a job. If you already have a job, don't forget to help others who seek to network with you.

Check Out Job Boards. Carpentry jobs can be discovered by checking out internet job boards that allow users to search by job type, employer name, geographic region, salary, and other criteria. Here are a few popular job boards:

- https://www.indeed.com
- https://www.monster.com
- https://www.glassdoor.com
- https://www.linkedin.com
- https://www.usajobs.gov (U.S. federal government job board)
- https://www.jobbank.gc.ca (Canadian federal government job board).

Join and Use the Resources of Unions and Professional Associations. About 14 percent of all construction workers in the United States belong to a union. The main union for carpenters in the United States and Canada is the United Brotherhood of Carpenters and Joiners of America. In the United Kingdom, carpenters are members of Unite. Many countries have unions for carpenters and other trades professionals.

There are many benefits to union membership. Carpenters who are members of the UBC and other unions typically receive higher earnings, better benefits, and more job

Salaries for Carpenters by U.S. State

Earnings for carpenters vary widely by state based on demand and other factors. Here are the five states where employers pay the highest average salary and the states in which employers pay the lowest salaries.

Highest Average Salaries:	Lowest Average Salaries:
1. Alaska: $69,970	1. Arkansas: $34,810
2. Hawaii: $68,960	2. South Dakota: $34,950
3. Illinois: $62,380	3. North Carolina: $35,560
4. New York: $61,900	4. Mississippi: $36,290
5. New Jersey: $60,380	5. Idaho: $36,810
	5. Florida: $36,810

Source: U.S. Department of Labor

security than those who are not members of unions. Additionally, union membership provides you with access to training opportunities and leadership development programs. The UBC's Carpenters International Training Center, which features seventy classrooms, offers a four-day program for third-year apprentices, which teaches soft skills and educates them about the union and potential employers; a four-day journeyman leadership training program; superintendent career training, an eighteen-month classroom and on-the-job program; and other opportunities. Another perk is that unions offer a large network of people who can give you tips on landing a job or even direct you to job openings.

Professional associations also offer many job search and career development resources such as membership, networking events, training opportunities, and certification. Most countries have at least one professional association for carpenters or construction contractors. For example, major organizations in the United States include Associated General Contractors of America, Home Builders Institute, and the National Association of Home Builders. The Institute of Carpenters is a trade association for carpenters in the United Kingdom. Organizations such as the National Association of the Remodeling Industry provide certification programs. Carpenters who are certified typically earn higher salaries and have better job opportunities than those who are not certified.

How Much Can I Earn?

You won't get rich being a carpenter (unless you own a thriving business), but pay in this industry will put you solidly in the middle-class. And that's pretty good for a job that doesn't require a college degree. What's better: unlike college students, apprentices begin earning as soon as they begin learning and often don't rack up education-related debt. (The average U.S. college undergraduate has $37,172 in student loan debt, according to The Institute for College Access & Success. And The College Board reports that 11 percent of graduate degree recipients have $120,000 or more in student debt.) As an apprentice, you'll begin by earning between 40 percent and 50 percent of what trained carpenters make, and receive pay increases as you gain experience. The U.S. Department of Labor (USDL) reports that the average starting salary for apprentices is $60,000. You can also prepare for the field by working as a carpenter helper. They earn median salaries of $28,810, according to the USDL. Earnings for helpers range from less than $19,690 to $43,030 or more.

Average Earnings

Carpenters are not the highest-paid trades workers (that honor goes to electricians, plumbers, pipefitters, boilermakers, pile-driver operators, and elevator installers and repairers), but they earn average annual salaries of $48,340, according to the USDL. This puts them right in the range of the average pay ($47,580) for all construction trades workers. Ten percent of carpenters (typically those without much experience) earn $27,070 a year.

The USDL reports the following average annual earnings for carpenters by employer:

- Other heavy and civil engineering construction, $56,820;
- Nonresidential building construction, $52,670;
- Other specialty trade contractors, $51,070;

■ *Contractors with successful businesses can earn $90,000 to $200,000 or more a year. Above, a contractor uses a nail gun to attach window trim.*

- Building finishing contractors, $50,370;
- Residential building construction, $45,420;
- Foundation, structure, and building exterior contractors, $45,090.

Top Earners

The top 10 percent of carpenters make $79,480 or more, according to the USDL. You'll make the big bucks if you're very experienced and highly-skilled, supervise or manage other workers, or live in a big city or other area where demand is high. Contractors with successful businesses can earn $90,000 to $200,000 or more, depending on the size of their companies.

If you're a member of a union, you'll often receive medical insurance, a pension, and other benefits. Self-employed workers must provide their own fringe benefits.

1. What high school classes should you take to prepare to become a carpenter?

2. What are the pros and cons of participating in an apprenticeship program?

3. How much can carpenters earn?

Research Project

Talk to carpenters who trained for the field in different ways (apprenticeship, college, carpenter helper, military). Ask them the following questions: How long did the training take, and what did it involve? What did you like and dislike about this type of training? If given the chance, would you train the same way to become a carpenter? What advice would you give to a young person regarding training to enter the field? Prepare a report that summarizes the interviews. Try to determine what would be the best training approach for you.

ON THE JOB
Interview with a Professional

Maria Klemperer-Johnson is the owner of Hammerstone: Carpentry for Women, LLC and Hammerstone Builders.

Q. What inspired you to get into this field? Can you tell me about your business?

A. Ever since I was a kid, I enjoyed building and making things. My dad and grandfather were hobbyist woodworkers, and I did projects with them, as well as took woodshop in middle school. In college, I would work on projects on school breaks, by reading books and getting help from my dad. But even as I recognized that this urge to create, especially with wood, was a strong part of my personality, I didn't think about carpentry as a legitimate career path. I studied computer science in college, where virtual creation helped assuage my urge to build. I minored in geology, where I was able to use both my body and mind in an outdoor setting doing field work. It wasn't until I tried and was unsatisfied with careers in both these fields that I realized the construction industry was a place where I could satisfy all these inclinations. I was finally able, in one place, to be creative, to be physical, to be outdoors, and to work with wood.

I recognized, before even entering the field, that it was male-dominated. And while I was able to make a path for myself with relative ease, eventually, the inequality of the field started to grate on me. That was when I decided to start Hammerstone: Carpentry for Women to introduce more women to construction and woodworking.

I now run two businesses: one is the school, and the other is a small contracting business. Our school offers short workshops teaching basic carpentry skills to women. Our contracting business does residential new construction and remodeling.

Q. Can you please tell me about a day in your life on the job?

A. One of the things I love about my work is that no two days are the same. Some days I sit in front of my computer all day answering emails, working on designs, doing bookkeeping, or writing estimates. Other days, I might be sweating in a t-shirt, hand digging holes for footers in the sun from 8 till 5. Or, I might be thinking through a complicated roof problem, working out the geometry with a pencil and paper and my calculator, and then cutting the pieces and installing them. Or, I might spend a day with a group of twelve teenage girls, teaching them how to frame a shed. Because I run my own company, I spend more time talking with people and solving problems in my head than I used to. But because I have a small business, I still get to put on my toolbelt and work with my hands.

Q. What is the most rewarding part of your job?

A. Before I became a carpenter, I studied computer science and worked as a programmer. While I liked the creative aspect of that job, I didn't like sitting all day in front of a computer screen. Then I went to graduate school to study geology, because I really liked being outside to do field work. However, I found I was not inspired by the research questions in that field; I really missed building stuff. When I started working as a carpenter, it was the perfect mix of everything I was looking for in a career. I love getting to work with my body and my mind, being outside, interacting with clients, employees, suppliers and designers, and creating beautiful, functional structures where before there was nothing.

Q. What advice would you give to someone who is considering a career as a carpenter? Are there any specific challenges faced by women in carpentry?

A. Carpentry is incredibly satisfying work, but it is not for everyone. If you are passionate about building, and are willing to work hard, then you should consider a career in the building trades. I work in residential construction, and learned my trade on the job. That is a great path for getting into custom homebuilding. If this is the type of construction you prefer, you should try to find a builder who does the type of work you like and who is dedicated to educating his or her employees. As you begin in the trade, you will be given more simple labor tasks. This repetitive work is a good opportunity to prove your work ethic. All work is valuable, and should be tackled with dedication. You should also take this opportunity to learn about the more complicated work going on around you. Watch, ask questions, and read trade magazines and books to build your skills. Doing projects on your own is a great way to hone your skills and to learn about the higher-level work carpenters do managing time, money, and resources while building.

Unfortunately, women do still face additional challenges getting into male-dominated trades such as carpentry. Most of these challenges stem from our preconceived notions about what work women are capable of doing. It can be tough to get a job with a contractor who doesn't believe you are capable of this work. And it can be difficult to have confidence in your abilities if you are constantly being told that you can't do this work. Also, because of deeply-seated cultural norms, young girls are still taught fewer hands-on building skills than boys are.
This puts them at a disadvantage when applying for construction jobs. My advice: if you are passionate about building, don't give up. Find a mentor. Find a nonjudgmental environment to practice your skills. Find an employer who supports you. Your might have to find a mentor in a different field, but there are women in all walks of life who have made their way in a male-dominated field, and in so doing have broken down barriers for those who follow. We are out here. Join us!

■ *Carpenters need strong communication skills because they must explain their work to customers.*

Words to Understand

blueprint: A reproduction of a technical plan for the construction of a home or other structure. Blueprints are created by licensed architects.

rehab: In the construction industry, to restore or rehabilitate a structure, typically a home.

royalty: A payment that is made to an owner for the use of copyrighted works, trademarks, franchises, or natural resources.

vulnerable populations: Those who are poor, the elderly, the homeless, and those who have serious, medical conditions.

CHAPTER 5

Key Skills and Methods of Exploration

What All Carpenters Need

Some aspiring carpenters think that all you need to do to be successful is to skillfully wield a hammer, tape measure, and a chalk line. But there are many personal skills and physical traits that you'll need to become a master carpenter, including:

Flexibility and problem-solving skills. Job sites vary. A carpentry task may be more challenging than expected. Building materials may arrive late or not match project specifications. And blueprints or job-site instructions may have errors. Carpenters must be able to "go with the flow" and solve problems to get the work done. For example, a prefabricated

■ *Carpenters must be in excellent physical shape because they frequently climb ladders, work at heights, and lift heavy building materials.*

door may be delivered to the worksite slightly oversized, and carpenters must shave it to make the door fit. Or an order of supplies may not arrive, and the carpenter must use what is on hand to keep the job on schedule.

- **Teamwork/interpersonal/communication skills.** Job sites feature people from many different ethnic, occupational, and educational backgrounds, so you'll need to learn how to work as a member of a team and interact effectively with others. Those who have strong communication skills (including listening skills) will have the most success on the job.

- **Detail-oriented personality.** Every action carpenters take affects the quality of the project. For example, if they incorrectly measure a window and its frame, leaks may occur during rainstorms.

- **Dexterity.** You'll need good hand-eye coordination to use hand and power tools, assemble intricate components, and avoid injury.

- **Ability to work independently.** You may be the only carpenter at a job site at times. In this instance, you need to be able to follow instructions without supervision, act ethically (no lollygagging or misuse of company equipment or supplies) and be a good time manager.

- **Physical stamina and strength.** If you wear a Fitbit® and work as a carpenter, you'll rack up some impressive numbers. Carpenters spend much of their days walking back and forth between job areas, climbing ladders or scaffolds (so good balance is important), stooping, bending, reaching, and kneeling. You'll also need physical strength because some tools, equipment, and material are heavy. For example, plywood sheets can weigh anywhere from 50 to 100 pounds (22.68 to 45.36 kilograms).

- **Business and customer service skills.** About 34 percent of carpenters in the United States are self-employed. Owning your own business can be rewarding, but you'll need to be skilled at customer service, marketing, cost estimation, bidding on new jobs, managing staff, planning payroll, scheduling work appointments, and performing other duties that keep your business on track.

Exploring Carpentry as a Student

Middle school and high school students will find it easy to explore carpentry. Do-it-yourself projects, classes, clubs, competitions, and information interviews are just a few ways to explore. Here are some tips to learn more:

Facts About Wood

More than 23,000 different species of trees are found on Earth.

The terms softwood and hardwood don't pertain to the softness or hardness of the wood on a tree, but to the leaves, seeds, and structure of the tree.

Wood-pulping by-products are used to create many different products, ranging from medicines and cosmetics, to cleaning compounds and artificial vanilla flavoring, to deodorants and hair spray.

There are about 747,000,000 acres (302,300,177 hectares) of forested land in the U.S.—or one-third of the United States.

There are approximately 3.04 trillion trees on Earth, or around 422 for each person on the planet.

Earth currently has 46 percent fewer trees than it did 12,000 years ago.

Sources: International Timber, American Forest and Paper Association, Yale University, Mother Nature Network

■ *Wood from oak trees is a popular building material.*

■ *Get hands-on experience by learning how to use a hand saw.*

Take Some Classes. There's no better time than middle school or high school to start learning about carpentry. Some schools offer complete curriculums in carpentry, where you'll learn basic framing, exterior and interior finishing techniques, side walling, and crafting and installing exterior and interior trim. In some programs, you might even get the chance to leave the school campus to work on construction projects such as garages, decks, home additions, and new homes. In shop class,

■ *Students in a woodworking class discuss a project.*

you'll receive an overview of the various types and qualities of wood, as well as learn how to sharpen saws, planes, and chisels; use a hand plane; cut a mortise and tenon joint; cut dovetail joints; and build and finish furniture. Math classes (particularly basic algebra and trigonometry) will provide you with the skills to be able to calculate volume and measure materials to be cut once you're on the job. Other useful classes include computer science and physics. If you plan to launch your own contracting firm, business, marketing, English/writing, and accounting classes will come in handy.

Join or Start a Woodworking Club at Your School. In such a club, you'll learn basic carpentry and cabinetmaking skills, as well as the safe and proper use of hand tools, table saws, band saws, drum sanders, routers, shapers for pattern cutting, and other tools. Your club might also get a chance to participate in state or regional wood-working contests where you can match woodworking wits with other teens to see who can build the best furniture, games, and even surfboards. Your faculty advisor can organize presentations by carpenters or tours of construction sites. No woodworking club at your school? Then start one with your classmates!

Participate in a Competition. Competitions are sponsored by schools, furniture companies, local park districts, or regional, national, or international membership organizations for young people who are interested in the trades. Here are some popular contests that will allow you to test your abilities against your classmates or students from around the country or world, make new friends, and develop your skills:

- **SkillsUSA** (http://www.skillsusa.org) is a national membership organization that serves middle-school, high-school, and postsecondary students who are interested in pursuing careers in the trades and technical and skilled service occupations. Its SkillsUSA Championships involve competitions in one hundred events. Students first compete locally, with winners advancing to state and national levels. A small number of winners can even advance to compete against young people from more than seventy-five other countries at WorldSkills International, which was recently held in Abu Dhabi, United Arab Emirates, and in Leipzig, Germany. SkillsUSA offers several carpentry-related competitions. For example, in the Carpentry Competition, students must successfully frame walls using wood or metal studs, cut and install rafters, install sheathing and/ or exterior siding and trim, and demonstrate knowledge of stair construction. Contestants are judged on their proper use of tools, equipment, and materials; accuracy; quality of workmanship; adherence to safety principles; and ability to read and interpret blueprints. In the Cabinetmaking Competition, contestants must build a small cabinet from materials and drawings that are supplied. According to the SkillsUSA website, "contestants are expected to read the drawings, lay out and cut the parts using a table saw, laminate trimmer, hand drill, hinge boring machine, and various hand tools. The parts must be accurately assembled, sanded, and adjusted to tolerances specified by the judges." SkillsUSA works directly with high schools and colleges, so ask your school counselor or teacher if it is an option for you.

- **Fresh Wood** (http://awfsfair.org/attendee-information/student-contests) is an industry-sponsored competition for full-time degree, diploma, or certificate-seeking students in an accredited high school or postsecondary school woodworking or related industry program in North America. The competition is held every two years in conjunction with the AWFS®Fair, with the next competition offered in 2019. Cash prizes are awarded. Projects must have been built in the two years before the competition. Event categories include Seating (e.g., chairs, ottomans, benches, etc.), Tables (functional, decorative occasional

■ *Participating in carpentry competitions is a great way to explore the field.*

tables, gaming tables, etc.), Case Goods (bedframes, shelving and storage systems, dressers, desks, cabinets, etc.), Design for Production (designs ready for manufacture), and Open (there are no restrictions on style, materials, or percent of wood used).

- **Doug Mockett & Company Annual Design Competition** (http://www. mockett.com/design-competition). This architectural furniture component and hardware company sponsors an annual design contest to identify the most innovative furniture parts, components, accessories, and hardware. The competition is open to people of all ages and educational backgrounds. Winners receive cash prizes and **royalties**. To enter, applicants should send a write-up of their idea, a drawing (better), or a model (the preferred form of entry).

- **Skills Compétences Canada** (http://skillscompetencescanada.com/en/ skills-canada-national-competition). This nonprofit organization works to encourage Canadian youth to pursue careers in the skilled trades and technology sectors. Its National Competition allows young people to participate in more than forty skilled trade and technology competitions. In the Carpentry Competition, contestants are asked to build a structure by reading blueprints, measuring and laying out components, cutting material, framing the structure, and assembling the components. Additional competitions include those in cabinetmaking, other trades, and workplace safety. In addition to participating in the competitions, student attendees can visit a dedicated "Career Zone" that features exhibitors and participate in Try-A-Trade® and technology activities.

■ *Build a black pipe wood bookshelf.*

Build Something! One of the best ways to learn more about woodworking and carpentry is to try your hand at building a bookshelf, table, chair, or decorative item. Ask your shop teacher or woodworking club teacher/mentor to provide project ideas. YouTube is an excellent source of how-to videos. The following books offer good project ideas:

- *The Big Book of Weekend Woodworking: 150 Easy Projects,* by John A. and Joyce Nelson (Lark Crafts, 2005).
- *Woodworking Basics: Mastering the Essentials of Craftsmanship,* by Peter Korn (Taunton Press, 2014).
- *I Can Do That! Woodworking Projects,* edited by David Thiel and Scott Francis (Popular Woodworking Books, 2016).

■ *One of the best ways to learn more about carpentry is to build something.*

Tour a Construction Site or Woodworking Studio. Your shop teacher, school counselor or woodworking club teacher/mentor can arrange a tour of a construction site or other place where carpenters work. This will give you the chance to see carpenters at work and ask them questions about their job duties, the tools and

■ *Students tour a construction site to learn more about the duties of carpenters.*

building materials they use, and other topics. Some industry organizations (such as Associated Construction Contractors of New Jersey in the United States and Go Construct in the United Kingdom) arrange tours to educate young people about construction specialties. YouTube and the Web in general offer videos of tours of woodworking shops and construction sites.

Talk to or Job Shadow a Carpenter. Participating in an information interview with a carpenter is a great way to learn more about this career. In such an interview, you gather information, but do not seek a job. You might even get a chance to don safety gear and use some basic tools. You'll find that many carpenters are happy to discuss their careers. Here are some questions to ask during the interview:

- Can you tell me about a day in your life on the job?
- What's your work environment like? Do you have to travel for your job?
- What are the hardest tools to use?
- What do you do to keep yourself safe on the job?

■ *Job shadowing a carpenter can teach you a lot about a career in the field. Above, a high school student tries his hand at woodworking during his job shadowing experience.*

- What are the most important personal and professional qualities for people in your career?

- What do you like best and least about your career?

- What is the future employment outlook for carpenters? How is the field changing?

- What can I do now to prepare for the field (classes, activities, projects, etc.)?

- What do you think is the best educational path to becoming a carpenter?

Consider job shadowing a carpenter. In this activity, you follow a carpenter around for a few hours or even an entire day on the job. You can ask questions, observe him or her as they build a home or a set of kitchen cabinets, and check out the tools of the trade and work environment.

Unions (such as the United Brotherhood of Carpenters and Joiners of America) and professional associations, as well as your school counselor, shop teacher, and family or friends who know carpenters, can help you arrange information interviews or job shadowing experiences. You could also try contacting a carpenter on LinkedIn (https://www.linkedin.com) to request such an arrangement.

Watch Television Shows. There are countless shows on television, cable, and the internet that show carpenters at work and the big picture of a building being **rehabbed** or built from scratch. Here are a few to check out:

- *This Old House:* http://www.pbs.org/show/old-house
- *Holmes on Homes:* http://www.hgtv.com/shows/holmes-on-homes
- *The Woodwright's Shop:* http://www.pbs.org/woodwrightsshop
- Many shows on HGTV: http://www.hgtv.com/shows

Help Out and Learn. What activity allows you to do good, while learning a skill? If you answered "volunteering," you're correct. There are many opportunities to learn about carpentry by volunteering with a local or other community group that repairs homes damaged by natural disasters such as hurricanes and tornados, builds or repairs homes for senior citizens, and offers woodworking/carpentry services to others who need a helping hand. Through your interactions with carpenters and other trades professionals who are volunteering their time, you might even make a connection that leads to a job once you graduate from technical school or complete an apprenticeship.

One noteworthy organization is Habitat for Humanity, which operates in nearly 1,400 communities across the U.S. and in more than seventy countries around the world to build affordable housing and repair existing homes for those in need. Through its Youth Programs (https://www.habitat.org/volunteer/near-you/youth-programs), Habitat for Humanity offers volunteer opportunities for those age five to forty. If you're in high school or college, you can start a Habitat chapter at your school.

Once you become an apprentice carpenter, you should consider volunteering with organizations such as Builders Without Borders (https://builderswithoutborders.com).

This Canadian-based nonprofit provides project management and construction expertise to help rebuild or construct safer homes, medical and community facilities, and schools for **vulnerable populations** in need and following natural disasters. It has participated in more than fifty projects in countries such as Turkey, India, Sri Lanka, Pakistan, Laos, India, Algeria, Ghana, the Philippines, and Haiti.

Sources of Additional Exploration

Contact the following organizations for more information on education and careers in carpentry:

Associated General Contractors of America

703-548-3118
info@agc.org
http://www.agc.org

Home Builders Institute

202-371-0600
contacthbi@hbi.org
http://www.hbi.org

National Association of Home Builders

800-368-5242
info@nahb.org
https://www.nahb.org

Timber Framers Guild

855-598-1803
info@tfguild.org
http://www.tfguild.org

United Brotherhood of Carpenters and Joiners of America

http://www.carpenters.org

1. Why is it important for a carpenter to be in good physical shape?

2. What classes should you take in school to prepare to become a carpenter?

3. What is SkillsUSA and what does it offer to students?

Research Project

Learn More About the Different Carpentry Specialties

Set up information interviews with carpenters who work in different job settings—such as building construction, home repair, highway construction, and furniture making. Ask the questions provided in the chapter and create a chart with a summary of their answers. Which specialty sounds like the best fit for your skills and personality? Learn as much as you can about this specialty.

■ *Many carpenters are nearing retirement age, which is creating many new opportunities for young people who like to work with wood and build things.*

Words to Understand

economy: Activities related to production, consumption, and trade of services and goods in a city, state, region, or country.

Great Recession: A period of significant economic decline worldwide, beginning in December 2007 and ending in June 2009, in which many banks failed, the real estate sector crashed, trade declined, and many people lost their jobs.

infrastructure: In relation to the construction industry, the systems of a city, region, or nation such as communication, sewage, water, transportation, bridges, dams, and electric.

3-D printer: A machine that manufactures three-dimensional solid object from a digital file. A 3-D printer can make anything from tools and toys, to metal machine parts and building fixtures, to stoneware and even food.

CHAPTER 6

The Future of the Carpenter Occupation

The Big Picture

Some people describe carpenters as the first people at a construction site when a project begins, and the last to leave it when it is completed. That just goes to show the key role they play in the construction industry. Another factor that suggests a good employment outlook is that it is difficult to automate most carpenter duties. They make dozens of decisions during a typical workday—selecting the right piece of veneer for a specific setting, determining how to stay on schedule if the wrong type and size of wood was delivered, talking with construction managers and other trades workers to make changes in the design—that it would be difficult for a robot to take over.

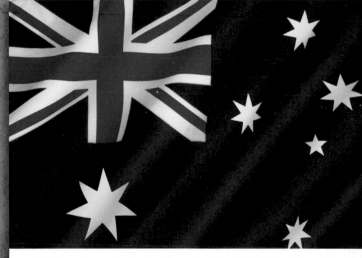

■ *There is a shortage of carpenters in Australia.*

As a result, there will always be demand for carpenters. But despite the steady need for carpenters and other trades workers, there's a shortage of skilled professionals in some countries. Many Baby Boomers are retiring from these trades, and young people aren't entering the

■ *Many carpenters will be needed to work on infrastructure projects, such as road repair.*

construction industry in big enough numbers to replace them. Some young people have been convinced that a four-year degree is the only path to a well-paying and rewarding career. Skilled trades workers will tell you that this is not true. They cite competitive salaries (carpenters earn salaries that match, or even exceed, those of people in some white-collar professions); the rewarding, constantly changing work environment; good advancement opportunities; and the ability to be your own boss (if you work as a contractor) as just a few reasons to become a carpenter.

But let's get back to the employment picture. Carpenters and other skilled trades workers are in short supply across the world, according to the human resource consulting firm ManpowerGroup. Globally, workers in the skilled trades were cited by employers as the most in-demand occupational field. By continent or region, skilled trades workers topped the most in-demand list in the Americas, Europe, the Middle East, and Africa. They ranked fourth in the Asia-Pacific region.

The recruitment firm Michael Page recently conducted research to determine demand for specific careers by country. It found that there is a shortage of carpenters in Canada, Norway, and Australia. In Canada, it's estimated that 44,600 carpenters will be needed over the next decade to replace those who will retire, according to the labor market research firm BuildForce Canada.

■ *Learn about disaster relief opportunities for carpenters with Team Rubicon.*

Employment for carpenters in the United States is also predicted to be good. Job opportunities are expected to grow by 6 percent during the next decade, according to the U.S. Department of Labor (USDL). There will be many new jobs for carpenters because of the following factors:

- The profession is very large—nearly one million—and there will be many new jobs, as well as a need to replace those leaving the occupation.

- Many Baby Boomer carpenters are approaching retirement age, and there are currently not enough trainees to fill replacement needs.

- New job growth in the construction industry. Approximately 1.5 million people left the U.S. construction industry during the **Great Recession**, and many did not come back. This has created a worker shortage. The construction industry has now rebounded strongly, and demand is growing for carpenters to work on new construction projects. Job opportunities for carpenters in the construction industry are expected to grow by nearly 8 percent during the next decade.

- Natural disasters, such as the devastating hurricanes that hit Texas, Louisiana, Florida, and the Caribbean in 2017, will necessitate considerable rebuilding operations that require the services of carpenters.

- Many roads, bridges, and other types of **infrastructure** are in fair or poor shape in the United States and around the world. In fact, America's roads received a letter grade of "D," its dams a "D," and its bridges a "C+," according to the Infrastructure Report Card from the American Society of Civil Engineers.

Women in the Carpentry Trades

Women make up about 47 percent of the U.S. workforce, but only 1.5 percent of carpenters. Construction industry movers and shakers, trade unions such as the United Brotherhood of Carpenters (UBC), and associations are trying to increase the number of women entering this exciting and rewarding career by hosting job fairs and offering open houses at training centers, founding support groups, and establishing pre-apprenticeship and mentorship programs. "The work doesn't care if you are a man or a woman, as long as you have the skills and can work hard," said Sue Schultz, outreach coordinator for the Northeast Regional Council of the UBC, in an article about outreach programs to women in *Carpenter Magazine.*

Here are a few organizations that exist to support women in the field of carpentry and the construction industry:

- The National Association of Home Builders (http://www.nahb.com) offers a Professional Women in Building group. Members receive *Building Women* magazine, networking opportunities, and the chance to apply for scholarships.

- United Brotherhood of Carpenters and Joiners of America's Sisters in the Brotherhood (SIB, https://www.carpenters.org/sisters-in-the-brotherhood) helps women obtain craft training and develop leadership skills, provides mentoring, and publishes the *SIB Tips* newsletter.

- The National Association of Women in Construction (NAWIC, http//www.nawic.org) offers membership, an annual meeting, and scholarships. It also publishes *The NAWIC IMAGE.*

- The Canadian Association of Women in Construction (http://www.cawic.ca) offers membership, a mentoring program, networking events, and a job bank at its website.

Overall, U.S. infrastructure received a "D+." Carpenters will be needed to help repair existing infrastructure and construct new roads and other transit systems, bridges, and dams. It's important to note, though, that the number of new infrastructure projects is tied to available funding from state and federal governments. The USDL reports that employment for carpenters in highway, street, and bridge construction is expected to grow by more than 12 percent during the next decade. Especially strong demand will occur in utility system construction.

- There's growing demand for green construction practices—the planning, design, construction, and operation of structures in an environmentally responsible manner. Green construction, or green building, stresses energy and water efficiency, the use of eco-friendly or fewer construction materials (when possible), indoor environmental quality, and the structure's overall effects on its site or the larger community. Green carpenters are knowledgeable about advanced framing techniques that use less wood and increase energy efficiency, building components that can support wind turbines or solar cells, and how to work with reclaimed lumber or alternate (non-wood) building materials.

■ *View an interview with a groundbreaking female carpenter.*

New Technologies

The construction industry has changed greatly in the last several decades. Construction sites of the past were filled with a tangle of electric cords leading to various power tools, workers holding manual tape measures, and piles of paper blueprints flapping in the wind. Today, many construction workers use battery-powered tools, measurements are made with the help of laser devices and computers, blueprints are reviewed on laptops and tablet computers, construction managers use cloud project management software, and, at some sites, **3-D printers** manu-

■ *Significant efforts are being made to encourage women to pursue careers in carpentry. Above, a female carpenter uses a belt grinding machine.*

facture parts and components, and drones fly overhead to assess the progress of construction.

These changes have also affected carpenters. They now use digital laser measuring devices to calculate area, volume, and more at the push of a button, and read blueprints on tablet computers or by using smartphone apps. Technology has also changed the way in which people train for the field. Apprentices in many programs must have their own laptop computers. Some union training centers have computer labs for apprentices to view training simulations. As a result, carpenters need to know how to use computers and be comfortable with information technology.

If you plan to operate your own contracting business, you'll need to become an expert at using office management software such as Microsoft Excel and Word. You'll need to attract customers, so internet and social media proficiency is also necessary. Finally, you should become familiar with building information modeling software, a computer application that uses a 3-D model-based process to more efficiently plan, design, build, and manage buildings and infrastructure.

These new types of technology might seem daunting, but you'll need to learn them quickly because more innovations are on the way. Technology is rapidly changing the way the construction industry works, and you'll need to stay on the cutting-edge of technology to be successful.

Challenges to Employment Growth

While it's a good time to be a carpenter, several developments may limit employment growth. If the **economy** weakens and another recession occurs, consumers will spend less on home remodeling, funding for construction projects will decrease, and governments will have less money to spend on constructing new buildings and repairing or expanding infrastructure. As a result, demand for carpenters will slow—although there will always be a need for people to repair and build homes and other structures, regardless of the strength of the economy.

Demand for carpenters is also tied to government policy. More carpenters will be needed if the government sets aside funds to pay for infrastructure repair or expansion and energy efficiency and alternative energy projects. If funding is cut, there will be fewer jobs for carpenters and other trades workers.

Job opportunities for carpenters may also decline because of the growing use of modular and prefabricated components such as walls, stairs, roof assemblies,

■ *More carpenters are using technology to do their jobs. Above, two carpenters use a laptop computer to review project blueprints.*

and complete bathrooms. These components are manufactured offsite, and then assembled and installed onsite by carpenters. The use of prefabricated components reduces the time it takes to build a house and the number of carpenters needed on a job.

Finally, it's important to remember that demand for all occupations ebbs and flows based on supply and demand. If many people decide to become carpenters, worker shortages will evaporate and there will be a glut of carpenters. In this instance, a carpenter may have to relocate to a city or region that is still experiencing worker shortages to find a job.

■ *View a video that provides information on why a career as a carpenter is such a great choice.*

In Closing

Is a career as a carpenter in your future? If you like working with your hands, using technology, solving problems, and making people happy by building homes, bridges, and roads, the answer is yes. And the good pay (top earners in the U.S. make $80,000 or more annually) and promising employment prospects worldwide make this career an appealing option for those who don't want to pursue a four-year degree. I hope that you'll use this book as a starting point to discover even more about a career as a carpenter. Talk to carpenters about their careers and shadow them on the job, use the resources of professional organizations and unions, and build a table, shelf, or birdhouse at home to learn more about the field and develop your skills. Good luck on your career exploration!

Did You Know?

- About 945,400 carpenters are employed in the United States. Twenty percent work in residential building construction, 12 percent are employed in nonresidential building construction, and 11 percent are employed by building finishing contractors.
- Approximately 33 percent of carpenters are self-employed.
- About 9 percent of workers in the construction industry are women.

Source: U.S. Department of Labor

Text-Dependent Questions

1. Why are employment prospects good for carpenters?

2. What types of technology do carpenters use to do their jobs?

3. What are some developments that might slow employment for carpenters?

Research Project

Learn more about green construction by visiting https://www.bls.gov/green/construction, https://archive.epa.gov/greenbuilding, and https://new.usgbc.org. Write a report about the pros and cons of using green construction methods and present it to your class.

apprentice: A trainee who is enrolled in a program that prepares them to work as a skilled trades worker. Apprentices must complete 2,000 hours of on-the-job training and 144 hours of related classroom instruction during a four- to five-year course of study. They are paid a salary that increases as they obtain experience.

apprenticeship: A formal training program that often consists of 2,000 hours of on-the-job training and 144 hours of related classroom instruction per year for four to five years.

bid: A formal offer created by a contractor or trades worker that details the work that will be done, the amount the company or individual will charge, and the time frame in which the work will be completed.

blueprints: A reproduction of a technical plan for the construction of a home or other structure. Blueprints are created by licensed architects.

building codes: A series of rules established by local, state, regional, and national governments that ensure safe construction. The National Electrical Code, which was developed by the National Fire Protection Association, is an example of a building code in the United States.

building information modeling software: A computer application that uses a 3D model-based process that helps construction, architecture, and engineering professionals to more efficiently plan, design, build, and manage buildings and infrastructure.

building materials: Any naturally-occurring (clay, rocks, sand, wood, etc.) or human-made substances (steel, cement, etc.) that are used to construct buildings and other structures.

building permit: Written permission from a government entity that allows trades workers to construct, alter, or otherwise work at a construction site.

community college: A private or public two-year college that awards certificates and associate degrees.

general contractor: A licensed individual or company that accepts primary responsibility for work done at a construction site or in another setting.

green construction: The planning, design, construction, and operation of structures in an environmentally responsible manner. Green construction stresses energy and water efficiency, the use of eco-friendly construction materials (when possible), indoor environmental quality, and the structure's overall effects on its site or the larger community. Also known as **green building**.

inspection: The process of reviewing/examining ongoing or recently completed construction work to ensure that it has been completed per the applicable building codes. Construction and building inspectors are employed by government agencies and private companies that provide inspection services to potential purchasers of new construction or remodeled buildings.

job foreman: A journeyman (male or female) who manages a group of other journeymen and apprentices on a project.

journeyman: A trades worker who has completed an apprenticeship training. If licensed, he or she can work without direct supervision, but, for large projects, must work under permits issued to a master electrician.

Leadership in Energy and Environmental Design (LEED) certification: A third-party verification that remodeled or newly constructed buildings have met the highest criteria for water efficiency, energy efficiency, the use of eco-friendly materials and building practices, indoor environmental quality, and other criteria. LEED certification is the most popular green building rating system in the world.

master trades worker: A trades professional who has a minimum level of experience (usually at least three to four years as a licensed professional) and who has passed an examination. Master trades workers manage journeymen, trades workers, and apprentices.

prefabricated: The manufacture or fabrication of certain components of a structure (walls, electrical components, etc.) away from the construction site. Prefabricated products are brought to the construction site and joined with existing structures or components.

schematic diagram: An illustration of the components of a system that uses abstract, graphic symbols instead of realistic pictures or illustrations.

self-employment: Working for oneself as a small business owner, rather than for a corporation or other employer. Self-employed people are responsible for generating their own income, and they must provide their own fringe benefits (such as health insurance).

smart home technology: A system of interconnected devices that perform certain actions to save energy, time, and money.

technical college: A public or private college that offers two- or four-year programs in practical subjects, such as the trades, information technology, applied sciences, agriculture, and engineering.

union: An organization that seeks to gain better wages, benefits, and working conditions for its members. Also called a **labor union** or **trade union**.

zoning permit: A document issued by a government body that stipulates that the project in question meets existing zoning rules for a geographic area.

zoning rules: Restrictions established by government bodies as to what type of structure can be built in a certain area. For example, many cities have zoning rules that restrict the construction of factories in residential areas.

Index

Photo Credits

Cover: Gpointstudio | Dreamstime.com

Title Page: Gpointstudio | Dreamstime.com

7: Tatiana Kasantseva | Dreamstime.com

9: Blackford | Dreamstime.com

10: Steven Frame | Dreamstime

11: Jeffrey Banke | Dreamstime

14: Monkey Business Images | Dreamstime

17: Sbukley | Dreamstime

18: Monkey Business Images | Dreamstime

19: Lastdays1 | Dreamstime

21: Gautier Willaume | Dreamstime

23: Juan Moyano | Dreamstime

24–25: Tonny Wu | Dreamstime

24: Brandont | Dreamstime

24: Agg | Dreamstime

24: Phfw22 | Dreamstime

27: Mira Agron | Dreamstime

27: Saša Prudkov | Dreamstime

27: Dtfoxfoto | Dreamstime

29: Andreblais | Dreamstime

29: Dpproductions | Dreamstime

30: Monkey Business Images | Dreamstime

31: Alexander Raths | Dreamstime

32: Monkey Business Images | Dreamstime

35: Stanislav Komogorov | Dreamstime

37: Monkey Business Images | Dreamstime

39: U.S. Department of Defense

44: Christina Richards | Dreamstime

48: Iakov Filimonov | Dreamstime

49: Steven Frame | Dreamstime

51: Milkas28007 | Dreamstime

52: Wavebreakmedia Ltd. | Dreamstime

54: Sergei Butorin | Dreamstime

56: Greg Epperson | Dreamstime

57: Goodluz | Dreamstime

58: Goodluz | Dreamstime

61: Les Cunliffe | Dreamstime.com

62: Didesign021 | Dreamstime

63: Steve Allen | Dreamstime

64: Rainer Klotz | Dreamstime

68: Robert Kneschke | Dreamstime

69: Syda Productions | Dreamstime

74: Dzmitri Mikhaltsov | Dreamstime.com

Further Reading & Internet Resources

Gibbs, Nick. *The Real Wood Bible: The Complete Illustrated Guide to Choosing and Using 100 Decorative Woods.* Rev. ed. Richmond Hill, O.N. Canada: Firefly Books, 2012.

Korn, Peter. *Woodworking Basics: Mastering the Essentials of Craftsmanship.* Newtown, Conn.: The Taunton Press, 2014.

Nelson, John A., and Joyce Nelson. *The Big Book of Weekend Woodworking: 150 Easy Projects.* New York: Lark Crafts, 2005.

Thiel, David, and Scott Francis (eds.). *I Can Do That! Woodworking Projects.* 3rd ed. New York: Popular Woodworking Books, 2016.

Internet Resources

https://www.carpenters.org/citf-training/citf-training-programs/career-connections: This website from the United Brotherhood of Carpenters and Joiners of America provides information on its Career Connections Program for high school students.

http://www.careersinconstruction.ca/en/career/carpenter: This website from BuildForce Canada provides information on job duties, training, and salaries for carpenters. It also features interesting videos depicting apprentices and women carpenters.

http://careers.abc.org: Visit this website for information on training programs for carpenters.

https://www.bls.gov/ooh/construction-and-extraction/carpenters.htm: This article from the *Occupational Outlook Handbook* provides information on job duties, educational requirements, salaries, and the employment outlook for carpenters.

http://www.byf.org: This web initiative of the National Center for Construction Education and Research offers overviews of more than thirty careers in the trades, videos of trades workers on the job, and much more.

About the Author

Andrew Morkes has been a writer and editor for more than 25 years. He is the author of more than 20 books about college-planning and careers, including many titles in this series, the *Vault Career Guide to Social Media*, and *They Teach That in College!?: A Resource Guide to More Than 100 Interesting College Majors*, which was selected as one of the best books of the year by the library journal *Voice of Youth Advocates*. He is also the author and publisher of "The Morkes Report: College and Career Planning Trends" blog.

Video Credits

Chapter 1: A carpenter discusses his job duties, necessary skills, and work environment: http://x-qr.net/1HVB

Check out carpenters working in a variety of jobs: http://x-qr.net/1FM1

Learn more about the variety of job duties for carpenters, required skills, salaries, and training: http://x-qr.net/1H2N

Chapter 4: Learn about the benefits of training via an apprenticeship program: http://x-qr.net/1CvN

Learn more about the ins and outs of participating in an apprenticeship: http://x-qr.net/1FLe

A female apprentice talks about the rewards and challenges of participating in an apprenticeship: http://x-qr.net/1DJf

Chapter 5: Get some hands-on experience by learning how to use a hand saw: http://x-qr.net/1EE8

Build a black pipe wood bookshelf: http://x-qr.net/1Ewn

Chapter 6: Learn about disaster relief opportunities for carpenters with Team Rubicon: http://x-qr.net/1H7j

View an interview with a ground-breaking female carpenter: http://x-qr.net/1F4Q

Learn why a career as a carpenter is such a great choice: http://x-qr.net/1FPb